Carolyn,

You are pure magic
dreams are your gift. You
have. Now is the time to create
them. Be nurtured & nurture
self as it grows your creativity.
I am grateful for having
the pleasure to cross
your path

Always available
Much love
Maria C
5/30/19

SUPPORT
NATIVE
HUMANITARIAN

Maria Crank is on a mission to make the collective reality more positive for all. Here to help humanity heal by increasing awareness and reconnecting with our spirituality

IT IS TIME TO HEAL HUMANS

YOUTUBE
Oracle EarthWarrior

VOCAL.MEDIA
Maria Crank

INSTAGRAM
Enerwe11

<u>Autobiography</u>

I am Maria Shantel Crank. Thirty-two, I was born in the best season of all, Capricorn season. Saturday, January the eleventh nineteen eighty- six my existence began in this planetary realm. Born in Charlotte, North Carolina. The first child born to young high school sweethearts newly married, Mario Crank of Chester, South Carolina and Beverley Bost of Newark, New Jersey. Charlotte, as my early memories provide, represented a fantastic blend of the past, present, and the idealized future of the new age world and its effects. Both the good and the bad. I was born and raised in the era of truths therefore at times I am remiss to this era of pretending.

My father is a man of humble means, where hard work was the fruits of your labor and labors were hard. The eleventh child, my father was the youngest. Born on Native soil, a small farm and home on land named of his own, "Crank's Dr", was the center of his very early childhood. His mother passed when he was twelve and father at the age of seventeen. Relocated to the 'city' to live with older siblings my father was one of the early "transplants" to Charlotte. All my life my father's love has been warm, supportive, caring and protective. I am THE daddy's girl.

My mother is the fourth of five children born to North Carolinians up-north trying to get a better start. A cold fast rough city in Jersey was my mother's upbringing until returning to the south in high school. Very outspoken and surrounded by a multitude of family, my mother has forever spoken and acted as she pleased. The warmth of large families is apart of my point of reference as well as alcoholism, drug abuse, violence, mental health issues, and death. I was made aware of adult realizations very early in life.

As a child, I was considered academically gifted and educated as such. I was bused from my low- income neighborhood school to higher qualified schools. Charlotte Mecklenburg school system, to this day remains one of the most segregated public schools in our country. With my peers, I can't say that I ever recall genuinely fitting in. To children of color, I talked white and was weird. To children that lacked color at the end of the day I was "colored". Diversity became most apparent by my middle school years. Grades were never much of a concern, my behaviors, however were a different matter. Just as your ordinary teenager I had slight issues with the law, fights, and of course the opposite sex. I became pregnant with my first child at fifteen giving natural birth at sixteen. I graduated in the thirtieth percentile of my class with a G.P.A of 3.50 or above. I completed high school a recognized scholar, working, and as a mother.

My second child followed at the age of twenty and my third at twenty-five. I obtained my diploma in nursing in two thousand and seven. I was a Practical Nurse until two thousand and fifteen when I became a Registered Nurse. I have lived. To progress, I had to learn to process, move forward, and always love self. With aspirations to become a Nurse Practitioner of Psychiatry, I have always hoped to bring who and what I am to help others. Originally, I wanted to help those with more challenging existences to be able to cope with self. As I grew personally and more importantly Spiritually, I became aware that my Soul's purpose is to help heal humanity specifically by increasing our self-awareness. Currently enrolled in Energy Healing courses, I have aspirations to open a practice to more readily service and assist those in need while working in health care.

As a young woman in this world, I have dealt with so much, as we all have. Learning to progress and remain intact throughout this process is a challenge that I have witnessed first hand destroy. I am in this world not of it. I do not believe in the agenda of social media, rarely do I watch television, I get on line when I have questions, and comfortable with myself I am seldom moved with the masses. These choices are based on my personal moral compass and the effect I see of others as evidence of actions, behaviors, and mindsets. I sternly believe that knowledge needs to be spread evenly and widely. It is something that is free and needs to be shared. We have to evolve together.

For She Allows We

Written by

Maria Crank
RN-Certified Energy Healing
Practitioner

Table Of Contents

This was created for,
naturally becoming dedicated to,
my female replicas.

Foremost my first born.
Forever will she symbolize the birth of
the most purest and true reflection of innocence
and essence of myself .

I love the constant reminder that even I have
sweetness sprinkled in and throughout.

Because I love your existence and I believe through

guidance you will achieve all and create the most
highest ,amazing, holistically tuned you...

My path has not been easy. I am aware now, more than ever, it will forever be this way. I constantly pray for strength not only to endure, but progress through this fact. I have learned to respect my process. More important, I have learned to LOVE self.

The words that follow I pray will not only inform, guide,and strengthen.

I pray they direct change of thought.

For it is our thoughts that truly rule supreme.

Enjoy these Mind Spells

With love,

Maria

Move

W here do you go when
You don't know where you are
Where you are going or
How you are getting there?
ONE STEP AT A TIME.
Movement is life
In anything, with all things
If the result is negative, not beneficiary for self
One must move
Move forward
Move to the side
Move or change your perspective
Try anything that you have already not
And always
Reevaluate self
Understand what is the reason self is in this current state
B. R. E A. T. H. E
Remind self
You are capable
You deserve change
You can do all things
The force of will is with you

Patience is Beauty

One has to learn patience
It is required just about above all things
Again patience
The virtue in patience is not sparance of time
But control of idle self
Beautiful
Be gracious that you understand the meaning
Understand it should not hold value
Value beauty with respect
Realize it remains in the eye of the beholder
It truly is created
It is an illusion
You are real

Not Equivalent

Understanding there is a real differences between female
and male will change how you interact
We are not equal
As a woman you are Origin
Thus greater
Women have awareness that men choose to neglect
Woman is aware of a multitude of emotions and feelings
Man disregards them
Realizing mans created limitation should help one to
Understand how to get the optimum result
Of this much needed interaction
Be aware of these facts
Always
You are not weak
You are great

Somedays

Fuck pulling up
"Big girl panties"
Its take them bitches off
Slang'um some fucking where
Let that good pussy breathe
And carry on
How you please!!!
You are woman
Life comes from you
Learn to have control
Even when you have no control
Having control over self
Its emotions or feelings
Is the closest thing to omnipotence
Which is the control us humans desire

-because shit gets hard
It is always too much
And NO
They don't understand

Lead me Guide me
Strengthen me

Be humble to self
To Life
To the realization of greater things
Label that awareness as you wish
Whether that be a God or Spiritual Guide
Just know connectivity is required
For true and holistic
Understanding of self 's existence
Always self check
Attitude
Emotions
Feelings
Appearance
Image
Self Love
Self Value and
Worth

Mental Masturbation

Learn to be to self

Learn to be for Self
Learn to be alone
Alone with your own thoughts and feelings
What makes you feel the way you do and why
Be comfortable being alone in a crowded room
Learn to be your greatest fan
Compliment self
Love self
Adore self
Make time for self
Take time to be alone
This is needed
This is required
Encourage self always
All things you desire in your mind
Take time to create
You are as great as you
Believe self to be

Your Temple

Your mind, body, and spirit are the "trifecta"
Caress them with love and encouragement
Nurture them
Take time for them
Make time for them
Feed them with the nutrients they require
Positivity
Moisture
Unconditional Love
The requirements will grow and change as you do
Always take heed to these changes
If you value your temple first
All that follow will

Healing

You have to heal from within

Yes, you.
Self
It starts from inside
You have to let go
Wherever the source originates
It is now seeded in you
Free yourself
It will rot and soil you
Taint
Leave its mark.
Do not allow this
Healing can be hard
We are all equipped to complete the task
We all can be penetrated
We must accept this as our nature.
Understand this.
With active awareness you now possess
the capacity to guard self

Libra Season

Inside

Love has to begin inside in order to receive from any
external source
Love must first exist internally
External sources may seem as though love originates from
them solely
This is not completely true

YOUR interpretation of these things are what creates
significance
YOUR interpretation comes from your view of love within
You
Realize this and your interactions will better suit you
Feel better to and for you
There will be challenges with this indeed
There are many variables that can and will affect your
interpretation
however
It all goes back to self
When self loves self first
Regardless the realness required
The Will of self is met with determination, vigour,
and above all
UNCONDITIONAL LOVE
To maintain and restore balance
in self.

That is love
Self Love

What love should be

Love is individual

The allure of love is to find one that will mimic your idea of
love
We are all different
Therefore and of course
Love will be and is different for us all.
The beauty is finding your universal equivalent
One with different
perceptions; understandings; interpretations
Of love that blends with fluidity
Creating an equally reciprocating interaction.
It takes two
Efforts should be and have to be
Equal.
Both bringing different aspects to the equation.
Aspects unique in our own differences.
This effort should be focused on nurturing and maintaining this
interaction
That those involved continue
With a positive experience
As agreed upon
Unified

Yes you can heal

You can not heal all.

Remember,
It starts from within.
All are not made of the same things.
Some drain.
Learn when to disconnect.
You will be sought after for your energy
Value it
Protect it
Nurture it
Preserve it
Be real and know when to stop efforts
Understand all may indeed have hope
You however,
will not exhaust the whole of
YOUR energy to any one outlet.

VAGINA!!!

Yes, it is a fact
You have a vagina
It is an organ
She is very much alive
She should not render shame or guilt
She is not a secret
Nor is her soul purpose the sexual pleasure for man
She is not weak, with God strength she is strong!
She is a portal
The gateway to other dimensions
The only entrance to this world
You are a gatekeeper!!!
How blessed are you ?!
Respect her
Keep her clean
Value her
Support her
Guard her
PROTECT her
Learn her
You are her.

P.S
Caution
She touches souls

Balance

Too much of anything can be bad
Always be aware of the way you interpret and
how your interpretations make you feel
Also be mindful of the reason for this feeling
Be aware
Yes all feel
However
All do not interpret their feelings

Confidence

Look into your eyes

Looking deeply
Be aware of who is looking back
Feel your heartbeat pulsate through your eyes
Now say aloud

I love you
I love you
I love you
You are so beautiful
You are so strong
You are beyond amazing
You can make it

Repeat as many times as necessary

Leave Some for Self

Do not give all your

Energy
Light
Love
Essence
Soul
Mind
Body
Spirit

Into one thing.. Other than self and your God

You need these aspects of self
Without them who are you?
What are you?
How can you?
Yes they are amazing
However they are most amazing
When you possess them

Your Aspirations

Be they big or small. Here or there
Understand they are your creation and a reflection of you.
You must believe in them. See them take place
Vision them. Deeply within your core
Feel the warm sensation they create when thinking of them
unfolding.
Understand the path to these desires may be filled with
experiences that challenge your vision
Have faith that your vision remains
Have faith that you are on your path headed in that direction
Evaluate your direction and progress to ensure you are truly on
your path
In the event you realize you are not, have the strength to get
back on that path
Encourage yourself deeply and often
As you will be the one to obtain your goal
Understand your God is with you, supports you, and loves you
However, it will be you that creates the practical effort to
achieve these visions
Be humble and remain true to self
You can change location
You can attempt to change or alter aspects of self
However it is your will and desire inside that will accomplish all
you need
Your vision can not change with or for others
All our paths are unique and different
What works for one may not work for all..
Know you can
You Can

Walk In Purpose

Be aware

Do not go through life unaware of the effects of your actions.
You deserve good, positive, holistic experiences.
You do not want to find yourself in life,
dealing with the consequences of circumstances you can no
longer alter due to past events.
You can contribute to your future in your present.
Your present can be ruled by your past.
Do not allow this.
Be active and aware in the moment
Understand all is a matter of perception

Too Much Too Quick

Save some for you
All do not deserve
All can not tolerate
All desires are not in your best interest
We all desire different things
Understand what it is you desire
Are you truly receiving what you desire?
It is better to retain and ponder
than
Losing without understanding

Your Basket

Keep all, well most, of your eggs in your own basket
You control your happiness
You control how you feel
Do not give that self control to others
Recognize and acknowledge your control
so that it can not be taken from you
Understand that control
So in the event you have lost this
You are aware and regain

Done

You know how to tell you are over something
When you are around that something
It is shooting while you are in vibes reach
and you feel nothing
That oh so important something has been changed to a
nothing.
You have that power.
You can actually take nothing and create something
Learn to use your powers at will
It will make you stronger

Restraint

One must learn this

Whether or not one chooses to use
..completely up to the individual
However,
Women must know of restraint
In all things
This tool,
This energy,
This force,
Is a very powerful
It creates the atmosphere for the purest of clarity
With nothing in the way
full knowledge present
All that remains must exist as is
Intention revealed
The fruit of restraint brings a labor not many truly care to bare

Power

You are
The most deadliest
The most fierce
Entity on this planet.
Know that
Embrace that
Take comfort in that
Have pride in that
Never forget.
Always be aware
and
May you control that.
Besides,
You are a lady

Soul Shivers

Recognize your personal level of influence
How the external stimuli affects you
All are different
It is unwise to gauge self based off others
Understand your levels before another recognizes
As this can and will be used to move you
Do not give away your control
To that in which you can not control

The Nature of Mother

Olde to female

A_s

Imperfect
Irrational
Unpredictable
Unbalanced
And all thy may be at the time
Know you are origin
Therefore you are rare in creation.
This is your nature.
Like the seasons
Like the light of day and dark of night
Even man's creation time
This too shall pass
Be easy on self
Support and nurture self
You will get through
You always have
You always will

Front to Back

Always.
Progressive motion not regression.
Forward not reverse.
In all things
From cleaning that precious vagina
To life choices
Front to Back
Not back to front
Be thorough.
*Kiss Kiss

Purple Prayer

Prayer of divinity and all that is female power

Mastery of my senses
Power when weak
Ambition to move forward, be better
Control over my entity
Command I receive
Bring wealth to all my endeavors
Lead me to my greater self.
Humbly gracious,
Your Essence
Amen

With Love
To one of my greatest loves
Mow Mow
Mrs Daisy Dean Harris Bost

The amazing power of creation

We can create our own reality

You have the ability to create your own unique and amazing
eden
Or
Create your darkest deepest hell
A space where no one can reach
Even you have trouble finding way through
Take heed of this place
Remember the signs and clues that lead here
So that you stay away
In the event you are taken into this place
Remember you have the ability to get out
Always ask self
Does your current reality reflect your current idea of creation?

Timing

There does exist the instance in which
no matter how badly you are moved to speak
A sharp opinion containing
Invoked emotions and feelings
It will be best
meaning necessary
that you remain silent.
Make nor take any action
You do nothing.
Dually teaching self both
Discipline and Restraint
Secondly you learn patience
If you are constantly
"Doing"
"Saying"
"Trying"
All with equally disappointing efforts
How will you be able to recognize your
God's work?

Be beautiful without shame

You were created this way
Dance with life always
Always you dance with the possibility to create life
Be aware of this.
Understand you may be weak
Yet your strengths are unmeasurable
You are ambiguous
You do not have to choose
For this reason do not
Be soft
Be firm
Be gentle
Be rough
Be all things that are you
You lead to different dimensions and galaxies
Of course you are complex
There will be those who will try even succeed in gaining from
created disadvantages.
Be ready.
You are not a victim.
You are a cosmic fighter.
One whose genome has survived eons
And has no intention on becoming extinct anytime soon!

-WOMAN

Believe

Close your eyes
Envision your desired aspiration(s)
Open your
Mind
Heart
Essence
to this desire.
When warm with glowing light
Repeat...

Move Forward
I am free
I am unique
What I feel is true
What I feel is for me
This is the right time
This is the right place
I am ready
I am willing
I will succeed
I am blessed
Amen

Red Lipstick Stains

You will be used when obtained

And thought of only when gone...

This can be a sad truth
Make yourself aware of this fact
as to not become anyone's possession

P.S
You are in control.
You are origin.

Get the Message

DON'T get stuck on repeat.
EVER
With anything.

Listen

Hear that inner "voice" which may not be a voice at all
That feeling
That sense
In your core
Your chest
Those unexplained butterflies in your stomach
Pay attention to that
Grow communication with that
Trust in it
You can and always rely on this with confidence
Your best interests are here.

F.Y.I

Oh, and why yesssssss

Love
Beautiful
Amazing
Deep and full
Can't live without love...
It hurts too!
Bad.
Deep.
Stings.
Takes your breath away.
Like I need air hurts.
It scars as well.
Can also wound.
Even infect..
Loves power has all types of side effects

Here is a story.
Learn this lesson from me.

Cosmic Rides On..

You are my strength and you are my weakness

You are my frustration yet you are my solace
You are my clarity and you are my confusion
You are my distraction and you are my destination
You are my path yet you mislead me

Knowing these truths I should be aware that...
Understanding you are everything and nothing
is not simple comprehension
You are moving yet I brace
You are unfolding and I continue to cover
You are vibrational connection yet I disconnect motionless
You are reflective awareness and I am a mirror
Realizing this
Recognizing alterations from these facts

One should be aware that...
Understanding I am force and you are electromagnetic
Is not simple magnets attracting
Is love good or bad
Pro or con..?
The complex question has a simple answer
Love is neither good nor bad
The intentions of entities involved...
Different story..

Understand?

What is for you will be for you.
You will not need
to force it,
search for it,
hunt it,
nor
hold it
It will be for you.

Move baby move

Dance to the beat of your own drum

Be free with no conditions
Have less thought about where the beat comes from,
But more so the rhythm it creates in you
Focus on how warm and content the beat makes you feel
Have faith and know this beat is created with divine intent.
Just for you.
Dance on Love
Dance on

Honey Face to Sour tongues

Be sweet

Be just
Be balanced
Be all things you want to receive
Be all that you can for a positive interaction
Be aware of your output to ensure desired input
Be understanding
Remain self aware
You will receive more with honey than you will with lemon
juice.

You Mad?

Don't be a

bitter

Bitch.

Love,
Honey Face

Forgiveness

This is most important for you not them.
Realize what we
Remember, know, think and understand is all different
If you do not resolve and let go
These emotions and energies remain in us
Right down to our cells and core.
Our very essence
They will remain affecting us.
Even altering all we do and are.
Forgiving releases
Thus unbinding
Unchain yourself
We are not domesticated animals

For Shika

Just do it

It can be simple
Don't think
Just feel
Now let go
Release

This is how you forgive
Understand somethings just are
Realize how that effects you
Deal with that.
Start that process however
Release that emotion
That feeling
That energy
Create something new
Something positive
Something to focus and work towards
Occupy your thoughts and energy on the new
Often not easy
focus yourself knowing
You can
You will
Heal

For Shika

Need a Moment?

Recognize when it is time to be alone

Let this need come fulfilled by choice
rather than the consequence of the actual need it self.

Laughter

Laugh
Laugh hard and loud
Aloud
Laugh randomly
Laugh with all your might
Laughter cures

When you find yourself in the position where you can not laugh

Pray
Be restored and
Laugh

Yes dear, there is more than you see

Just as you are aware there is something beyond the clouds in
our sky
You HAVE to be aware that there is more to you than what
you can
See or feel of self
This physical body...
Feel
Sense
Become aware of that other part of self
That warm and comfortable part
Those thoughts
Likes and dislikes
All that makes you
This is you
Your spirit
Your essence
All that creates you
Your soul
Your energy
Your creation
The essence of creation that represents you
The divine creation that reflects the Divines capacity in creating
This is what others experience when they interact with you
This is what you nurture, grow, alter and at times
destroy when you interact and experience
You must of many things remember ...
(back to the top)

Blue Prayer

Harmony and peace be with me
Fill me. Warm me. Guide me.
Fill my dwelling, my living space
Bring joy to this place
Fill me with good intentions
May all my actions be first in my Gods hands
Amen

To Suga
From Von
Via
The Spirit
Amen

Our thoughts are powerful

Believe. Have faith. Remember

You are not alone
You are loved
You are supported
There are forces greater than yourself present and
willing to assist
These forces will forever be unique to you
Accept and allow this assistance
Connect with that help line
Communicate often with it
Trust in that guidance
Belief, faith and prayer.
These are more than important
They are required to maintain your essence
They focus our thoughts
Directing them to an abundant source
of love and assistance
that has all we require

Find your amen

Amen

Yellow Prayer

Devotional prayer
To the warmth and productivity
of positive energy

Devotion to positive energy

Pure energy
White light
Bringing fortunes glow
Quickly the positives of good fortunes energy fills me
Make me light, happy, and content with this new way
I ask positive and golden energy continue to attract to me
Amen

Telephone..TeTettelaPhone...

As with all communication
prayer does not necessarily have to be a quote from one specific
source.
As long as the communication is wrapped with respect and
humbleness,
the intent can always be unique to the sender and needs at the
time.

Pray on!
Pray on !!
You shall receive!!!

Do be careful of what you ask for
You just may receive
Also be mindful of the TRUE intent
Intention is the basis of all forms of communication

Receive your blessings

You have to be open to receive.

You must allow.
You will have to go places you didn't know existed
Enjoy and relax
You deserve it, yes?
Now be humbled and give thanks

Knock Knock, What's There?..

Doors are simple man made portals
This is true!
Think...
A door leads from one "place" to another
Same as a portal
Learn these simple understandings of DOORS

* Open the door to walk through it

* Ones own intent should be the force behind
crossing a doorway to yield most positive results

* Where one door closes another shall be open

* There are times when doors will have to be
closed so that you may open another

* Learn when to open and close doors

* A lady always closes doors behind herself

* A lady needs not break down doors therefore
she will not

* These doors are not real however the portals
they link are, always proceed with caution

Do Not Enter

One of the most alluring factors of the feminine influence lies
in desire, indeed
However, it is what desire leads to that holds undeniable
power
The illustration of the spark of creation as manifested in
feminine pleasure opens a portal.

This place unique for all yet unified in relevance
Subdues, Fills, and Conquers the essence of
PURE PLEASURE

Take heed to the knowledge of pleasures perceived taint
and its effects.
The purity in the reaction of pleasure is so intense
often negatives are taken from its reaction
As it seems
ones will does not exist in the presence of pleasure

Beware of this woman
Be aware of Woman
The Conqueror

You are what you are

There will be no shame in following facts

As woman you are feminine.
The word alone when spoken or thought of yields recognition
deeply rooted in all.
A reaction with frequencies resonating deep within.
So deep often rippling to the core.
Shock waves vibrating
throughout, back, towards, and within again.
A continuum.
Your connection to creation through your ability to create
elicits a heightened sense of emotional awareness.
An awareness whether known to you or not

is transmittable ...

Be aware of who and what you let tap in

Knock Knock..Again

* All doors will not be for you, as all paths are not yours

* Who said anything about keys?!

* Once some doors are opened only seals will keep them closed

* Once some doors are opened they can never be closed

* Whenever there is a knock on my door I do take heed however I ain't always opening my doors

* What knocks on your door ain't got nothing to do with mines

* Entrance through one door does not necessarily grant entrance to another or all

* Understand what opening the door alone truly means

System Check

It is important to exist in

positive, progressive and productive connections

Friends
Family
Coworkers
significant others
Siblings
Mentors..
All.
These connections have a direct effect on your being
Therefore and naturally
One should want to ensure the connection is a good one

If a connection is bad ...
Brings you harm
Discomfort or
Down to lesser state
Disconnect immediately!!!
Always remember
Self first
Self preservation

Animal kingdom rules
#beastmode

Silk like features

I am an intelligent being
My creation is divine
I am a sensual being
I create life therefore I must procreate
I accept this as who and what I am
I have no shame in the fact my sensuality creates life
I am universal
I am origin
I embrace my being
My pleasure and my comfort within my sensual state is
important to me
I value my being
I will guard and protect my being
Most of all I will shield my essence
I understand I control
Amen

There is Pleasure in Pain?

There will be pain before your pleasure
This pain should not be sharp
There will be pressure
Breathe..

Relax...
There should be trust
Fear should not exist in this moment
Allow
Open
Receive
The discomfort of pain should fade
There is this pressure
Allow it to be full
Allow it deep
Breathe..

Relax...
Rhythmic vibrations should create tides
Allow
Open
Receive and
Breathe..
Now go with the flow and let go

You Can't Ignore this 'Ality

Just as your most earliest experiences help shape

how you speak, interact and interpret others
They also affect how you express your uniqueness..
Your Personality.

All you experience also helps to shape your sexuality
Your sensuality.
This is one of the most personal forms of
Expression..
Reception..
Perception..
You have
Do not ignore this aspect of self
Have no shame in or who and what
you are as a sensual/ sexual being
Remember this is embedded in your nature by nature
Explore your sensuality
Respect it
Understand it
Nurture it
Grow it
Embrace it
Do all these things
FIRST
before you share it

Tube Pleasure

Looking to others and elsewhere
to understand what makes you fulfilled
is unnatural.
Allowing others to define or change
what satisfies or even dissatisfies you
is unnatural.
What others desire and enjoy
should not heavily motivate your personal fansies.
Be secure in love
Entrust yourself with trusting actions for self.
Ensuring exploration of self
not self exploitation of flesh

Read this Eleven times
For a strong sexual
Esteem

Let's Get Technical

Ex-ploi-ta-tion

Treating someone unfairly in order to benefit from their work
taking advantage, ABUSE, misuse, OPPRESSION

Making use of and benefiting from resources, utilization,
capitalization, "cashing in on"
Making use of a situation to gain unfair advantage for oneself

Do not allow yourself in any circumstance
To fit into these definitions
ESPECIALLY
When it comes to what makes you
WOMAN
As a woman you are one of the most valuable
RESOURCES
To our species

No Turning Back

Once they've been in...
They have been in there
This is fact regardless of how less you desire this.
It is true.
Always and forever it will be a fact.
Therefore do be very mindful
Of who and what you let in.
Love your mind , body, and soul
with the understanding they are all more valuable
than immortal gold

Leave Sex to Earthlings

Be out of this

World and connect

It is much better and more fulfilling

Physical Physical Physical
Shallow interactions and reactions coming from different
perspectives
combined into one Physical action
This is sex
Where left out in this cold world
the rod of man is once again welcomed
into the warmth of all there is,
Surrounded in the fluidity of love.
Where once filled deep and throughout
Alive with the vibrations of existence
Now alone with self
The entrance to the portal,
womans vagina,
receives and accepts.
Through this method, rarely is the intent
to travel into the womb reaching lands of fertility
Aka that space in between reality and all things unknown
All thought is focused on
Please that physical!

Keep that feeling going
The kinetics baby the kinetics!
May the force be with you
And oh thank universal laws for the force!
However.. There are times when
there is the need for more than just force
When entrance stops time
Breaths become rhythmic chants
Eyes unlock, dilate, and join
Thought does not exist
Momentum builds, drops, fades, and rises again
Energy begins to flow.
What organs?
These bodies do not exist
My God
the Universe is within and apart of we
Woman
We are creations template
How much better could existence get?!

The Motherboard

You are a transmitter

Do be cautious of who you allow to tap in
As you allow entrance you also agree to transference
You are them
They are you
Some linger and can stain
Some share too many connections
Bringing others energies with them
Do not forget the more connections you open
The more open you will be
Hold tight!
Don't leak out now!

Gift Wrap Indeed Speaks on the package

What you choose to garb, cover, express,
Yourself with does speak or represent not only how you feel
but how you value self...
Are you clean
Dirty,
Presentable,
respectful,
or do you just not give a #$%!
Intentional or not
how we choose and what we choose
to place on our bodies create and distract attention
Be aware of this

Just Walking around with Extra Life

Feminine entities have an amazing first hand perspective of
creation
One in which we not only first hand but actively participate in
nothing becoming something
This is where your deep seeded hope comes from among
things
When properly charged our properties produce life
As this life grows, becoming complex from simple means, we
nurture with our own flesh and blood
Protect with our bodies and prepare with our minds
This is why you nurture
This is why you give..among things
From the first flinch of new life to the ripe fullness and
expansion of creation
The capacity to witness before experiencing the sight,
The ability to understand life before it begins provides a unique
perspective of what we know to be creation and life
As ones body begins to be the single source of multiple fruit
Be empowered
Be great
Be humbled by your relevance
Hold your flesh
Be grateful
Be proud
Most of all be proud
You are doing exactly what nature asks of you

Learn that within darkness there is light
Never forget we all come from darkness full of light.
Always remember your womb is filled with the spark of
creation and the power of the universe.
You are the light.

Exchange

To give life
Surely you will know deaths icy, rigid, and gripping touch
You will definitely know
immeasurable strength,
moving humbleness,
and most of all
UNCONDITIONAL LOVE.
Of your
energy and blood
new life begins.
Made of creation
now in this world
New links are birthed
into the infinite cycle
called life

Fading pain into the pleasure of loving ...
Exchange

Tiling Your Seed

Once you start reproducing self
Let no human come before your seed.
Only your God is before your creations as source is their origin
Nurture your seed with LOVE above all things
as well as time
Recognize this new form of self
Understand it
Assist it in the current form of this world
Take responsibility for it
Expect, desire, and support your seed
be greater and do greater than self
Do all things in understanding
how blessed are you to have the ability to reproduce
YOUR unique genes
Solidify in your awareness that your seed is truly your
immortality

Name Calling are we?

Life is a bitch is that right?
A cold one huh?
Vicious did you say?
Hell on wheels?
Oh not Karma too!
There is no hell like who scorned?
A bitch is a what?!
All these references to female!
Then again call it like you see it
We are our actions
This includes your life
Your karma
Your efforts
Your benefits
Use this knowledge to always move with grace and realize
through your actions why yes there lies control of
Reactions

Throw a stone of sweet love into the pond
What kind of energy does it ripples carry?

Come to Jesus Meetings

Sit down

Be ready to get really REAL
Think of what your issues are
Remember how it began
Or
Try to link any possible common factors
If you find that either
Your lack of actions
Or
You actions themselves
Are constantly or consistently coming up
The issue is YOU
It be like that sometimes
Can't go back and erase past events
We can however start in this moment
Start making better choices
Start forgiving self
Start letting go
Let go!
Let it go!
Breathe.
You will be alright
You are alright
Be better
You are better

Focused

BE HUMBLE
Remain great
STAY TRUE to self
See others
Pay them no mind

Repeat Nine times !!!

I stay focused on me and mine

Tunnel Vision

If you believe in something focus your thoughts and energy
into this belief
It will come true because for you it is true
All things you imagine you can achieve
Start at anytime
You just have to start
Believe in what you imagine
Imagine the things you believe
Push
Keep going
Regroup
Learn to keep moving
When obstacles seem to block your way
Take the time to move them
If need be walk around them
Run through them
Just as long as you let nothing stop you from your goals
Be tenacious for yours
Have faith in yourself
Encourage yourself
Be patient with yourself
Understand self
Make sure self is aware
Realize you need to be your greatest
Most loyal
Support

You need it to Give it

Respect others

First respect yourself
Be kind to all
Start with you
Treat others how you want to be treated
How good are you to self?
Encourage and support love
You are loved

Orange Prayer

May I be blessed with sight
May I be assisted by flowing light
May I receive from all those assisting in opening the way
May I be flexible. Capable to receive
May I endure and hold faith when my path becomes obscured
May I understand the change of plans are for the greatest
good
May I recognize I have never left thy hands
May prophetic dreams be visions of your path
May I humbly obtain all that is for me
Amen

#AintShitFree

W hen acting out of necessity
actions become rigid and calculated.
PRESSED.
Always act in faith,
That all you need will be provided.
Your actions will be even, smooth, and REWARDING for your
provider
Understand the energetic exchange has to be even
With and for all those involved
One should not expect to receive having provided null

Remember control

Remember your will
Know your strengths
Realize that circumstances can change
You have
the will and the strength
To change, alter, or improve your situations.

Your past does not define
who or what you are
Or
who or what you will become.
Believe this
Understand the power in and of this fact
All that you have experienced makes the unique entity that you
are
Without these experiences you would not be you
Even the hard, unpleasant, and undesired experiences.
We can not erase these
when you can not accept these experiences realize you got
through.
They are apart of your experience
Not apart of WHO and WHAT you are

Joy Ride

Indeed there are times to sit back and enjoy the ride

There too exist instances in which
You need to take the wheel,
Break fast!
Let up off the gas,
There will also be times in which you need to FLOOR it!
When you know in your heart
inside your core
something is not right for you,
or not what you desire or want,
It may not even be what you need
YOU have to be the change

Do not sit back doing nothing
Complaining about everything

Caught Up?

Don't get "caught up" in the way of things
This world
Trends
People
Career
Even Self
Too much of anything can become perverse
When focus becomes obsession
One has a very limited view
Only focusing or giving attention to few things
Missing so much
Even a blessing or two
Remember to take the effort to loosen self
Release
Do nothing
Remind self of how well you are doing
Smile because of this
Breathe
Too often we get caught up in things
Enduring unnecessary experiences
END THIS

"Women just know how to suffer better"
Words from a successful pale male

I sat and thought of all I've been through...

How did I do it?!

Be ready for the cold
Keep the heat of love in your chest
Understand to some you are vulnerable
Embody the strength of this inaccuracy
Place no limits on self
As you are limitless
All your actions count
Be aware of that fact
You are more than what can be seen or touched
Feel that
When alone you have a regiment at your side
Know that
Trust in what you feel
Not what you see
Do not allow the illusion of sight to block your path or blessings
Be humble in your interactions
Implore brutalness with those who attack
Keep your eye on the goal
The goal is
To be a better you
Always

Realize you are blessed

Do not fear
Do not hold anxiety
nor hesitation when your blessings arrive
Accept and receive necessary change openly
All you gain is for you
Relax in the abundance of love
Allow and accept
Do not question your role
continue as you are with grace
Your actions are what lead to your blessings
Continue to move with faith
Be thankful. Show gratitude.
Be joyful
Be fulfilled
Be blessed
You are highly favored

It is not you

All are not happy with self
Therefore no they can not be happy for you
Many have never been encouraged
So no
They do not know how to support you
Several crumble to challenge
Of course they feel
"A certain way" that you push through
Too many only recognize negatives
Unfortunately no they do not see positive in anything
This has nothing to do with you
Remember this fact
Learn to be happy inside and with self
Learn to encourage and support self
Learn to take responsibility for how you feel
Making sure your feelings are not blocking you or others
Learn to focus on your positives
Learn to acknowledge positive
Learn to be positive

The Goal

As you grow and experience you will change
Be mindful of this
Be prepared for this
Accept and allow this
Your lifes lessons are for you to better yourself
Creating forward change
Change that will progressively enhance self
This is the goal
Backward change that causes regression is unnatural
This is not the objective of change in your life
These types of experiences you must be mindful of
One must not allow experiences to create
Bitterness, negativity, or harden self to the point of breaking
Throughout change one should be able to recognize self
If and when you find that you can not recognize
Who or what you are
Know that it is time for change
Forward change
Change that will progressively enhance self
This is the goal of change in your life
This is your goal

This world has long been tainted, rough, and cruel
Pureness, beauty, and ease do yet remain
You are in this world
You do not have to be apart of the ways of this world
For change you have to be change
As a woman
You are a natural healer
A nurturer
A creator
You are gift to this world
This world is in desperate need of all you offer
In order to provide for any
First, you must provide for self
Be the love
The support
The understanding
The patience
The unconditional love you require
By doing so a warm bright light of energy will flow
within and from you
Touching all you interact with
All you desire can and will be yours
Just as long as you
Love yourself woman
With love
Maria
12/31/2017

Self Reflections

CPSIA information can be obtained
at www.ICGtesting.com
Printed in the USA
BVHW030458160519
548399BV00007B/18/P